MARKETING
RESEARCHING & REACHING YOUR TARGET MARKET

by
LINDA PINSON
&
JERRY JINNETT

Published by

OUT OF YOUR MIND...
AND INTO THE MARKETPLACE™

Fullerton, CA 92633

MARKETING: Researching and Reaching Your Target Market
By Linda Pinson and Jerry Jinnett

Second printing: May 1989
First printing: April, 1988

Published by: **OUT OF YOUR MIND....**
               AND INTO THE MARKETPLACE™
               3031 Colt Way #223
               Fullerton, CA 92633

Cover Design by Linda Pinson

© 1988 and 1989 by Linda Pinson and Jerry Jinnett

All rights reserved. No part of this book may be reproduced or transmitted in any form with the intention of reselling such copies without written permission from the publisher, except for brief quotations included in a review.

Buyers of this book are licensed to use the forms included in this book in the course of conducting their business. The contents of this book, however, may not be reproduced for sale.

Library of Congress Catalog Card No: 88-90666

ISBN 0-944205-12-7
Printed in the United States of America

DEDICATION

This book is dedicated to the memory of E.C. "Jerry" Maroon and Wendell Jinnett. Their faith and encouragement have been our inspiration.

TABLE OF CONTENTS

PART I   RESEARCHING THE MARKET 3-52

CHAPTER 1: HOW TO SURVEY THE MARKET 7-9

EVALUATE CURRENT BUYING TRENDS 7
NEW PRODUCT 8
NEW SERVICES 8

CHAPTER 2: PROTECTING YOUR IDEA 13-17

DISCLOSURE LETTER 13
JOURNAL 13
COPYRIGHT 13
TRADEMARK 15
PATENTS 15

CHAPTER 3: THE USE OF QUESTIONNAIRES 21-30

FORMAT 21
TYPES OF INFORMATION 22
DISTRIBUTION 23
EVALUATION OF THE RESPONSE 25

CHAPTER 4: TESTING THE MARKET 33-35

PROTOTYPE 33
TESTING A PRODUCT 34
TESTING A SERVICE 34
LETTERS OF REFERENCE 34

CHAPTER 5: EVALUATING THE COMPETITION 39-41

FINDING THE COMPETITION 39
EVALUATING THE COMPETITIVE SERVICE 40
EVALUATING A COMPETITIVE PRODUCT 40
UNIQUENESS AND BENEFIT TO THE CUSTOMER 41

CHAPTER 6: FINDING YOUR TARGET MARKET 45-52

DEMOGRAPHICS 45
PSYCHOGRAPHICS 47
PUTTING IT TOGETHER 47

PART II REACHING YOUR TARGET MARKET....53-95

CHAPTER 7: POSITIONING YOUR PRODUCT OR SERVICE............57

CHAPTER 8: PRICING..61-68

CHAPTER 9: PACKAGE DESIGN..71-72

CHAPTER 10: METHODS OF DISTRIBUTION.................................75-77

CHAPTER 11: LOCATION..81-83

MARKET...81
SUPPLIES..81
LABOR FORCE...82
TRANSPORTATION...82
COMPETITION...82
COST...82
HOME - BASED..82
SHOPPING CENTER..83
INCUBATORS...83

CHAPTER 12: TIMING OF MARKET ENTRY..................................87-88

CHAPTER 13: ADVERTISING YOUR BUSINESS.............................91-101

MEDIA ADVERTISING..91
DISPLAYS, COMMUNITY INVOLVEMENT, AND NETWORKING..........93
TRADESHOWS AND EXHIBITS..93
DIRECT MAIL...93
TELEMARKETING...94
YELLOW PAGES..94
DISCOUNTS..94
PROMOTIONAL GIMMICKS..95

SUMMARY...105

FOR MORE INFORMATION..107-111

INDEX...113-117

INTRODUCTION

The development of a good marketing plan is essential to your business success. Your product or service may be in demand and be competitively priced. You may have found the lowest prices for your supplies and may have secured adequate financing for your business. All of these items will be of no value if you have not taken the time to identify your customers and found the means to get your product or service to them. The key word here is **time**. It takes time to research and develop a marketing plan, but it is time well spent.

There are professional level firms and individual consultants who can conduct market research for you. They conduct market surveys, compile the data, and make recommendations. This service may be too costly for the small or home-based business.

Don't overlook non-professional sources for help with market research. Contact the Business Departments of the Colleges and Universities in your area. Often students majoring in Marketing are required to do marketing surveys and prepare marketing plans as part of their coursework. There generally is a nominal fee. In return, you will be getting a marketing plan prepared by motivated, bright, and energetic students who will be graded on the project.

Another resource is S.C.O.R.E. (Service Corp of Retired Executives) which has been administered by the U.S. Small Business Administration since 1964. The purpose of both S.C.O.R.E. and the S.B.A. is to help the Entrepreneur get into business and stay there. S.C.O.R.E offers free, one-on-one counseling, seminars, and workshops. If you need help with marketing, you can be assigned to a counselor with expertise in that area.

You may choose to do your own market research and develop your own marketing plan. Most of the information you need can be found in your public or college library and in the publications of the Department of Commerce, the Small Business Administration, and the Census Bureau. Additional information is available from trade associations and their publications and through the Chambers of Commerce. By doing your own marketing research and developing your own plan, you will have demystified marketing. You will learn all there is to know about your type of business.

Marketing has been defined as all the activities involved in moving goods and services from the seller to the buyer. Marketing is **everything** you do to promote your business. It is your business card, your location, the way you present yourself, the attitudes of your employees. A person concerned with marketing must be consumer-oriented. View your product or service in an objective manner. Determine the identity of your business and carry it through your product design, advertising, and your promotional materials.

This book has been designed to take the mystery out of marketing. It presents a step-by-step format for developing your marketing plan. You will begin by conducting your market research. You want to survey the market, evaluate the competition, and identify your target market. Once identified, you develop a strategy for reaching that market. You will position your product and get it into the marketplace. A resource list is provided at the ends of chapters to give you additional information.

View the process of market research and planning as detective work. You are on the trail of the elusive "target market" and you won't get paid until you find them! The more "clues" or information you have, the more successful you will be in finding that customer and having the satisfaction of selling your product or service.

PART I

RESEARCHING THE MARKET

How to Survey the Market

Protecting Your Idea

The Use of Questionnaires

Testing the Market

Evaluating the Competition

Finding Your Target Market

1

HOW TO SURVEY THE MARKET

Evaluate Current Buying Trends

New Products

New Services

1 HOW TO SURVEY THE MARKET

In order to be successful, a business must know its market. Market research is an organized and objective way of learning about your customers. It involves finding out what a customer wants and needs and determining how your company can meet those wants and needs.

EVALUATE CURRENT BUYING TRENDS

A **trend** is a behavior or buying pattern that lasts between 5 and 10 years and is generally widespread. Current trends seem to be nostalgia, family closeness, unusual foods, quality products, self-help material, concern about health, aging, and the environment, and convenience. **Fads** seem to occur among smaller groups for only a year or two. The smart business person looks for the trends.

Don't underestimate personal observation. You can learn a great deal about the buying habits in your area by watching the purchases being made in the supermarket check-out line as well as at the stores in the mall. What specialty shops are opening? What colors seem to be popular? What books are on the best seller lists and what subjects do they cover?

We see the current trend toward family and nostalgia shaping what consumers buy. Popcorn sales and video rentals indicate the trend toward family evenings at home. "Home-made" packaged and easy-to-prepare foods combine convenience and nostalgia.

Trends can be anticipated by analyzing television. On the "Cosby Show," Bill Cosby began wearing multicolored, patterned sweaters. A trend was started and we now see these fashionable sweaters in stores, in catalogs, and in advertising. Television programs have a great influence in our lives. Watch them with a marketer's eye.

Reading the trade journals and publications for your field can also give you that "edge." The **Gift Reporter**, a trade journal for gift retailers, indicated in 1986 that there was an interest in products featuring dinosaurs. We now see stuffed dinosaurs, dinosaurs on coffee mugs, and dinosaur calendars. This may prove to be a fad rather than a trend, but incorporating dinosaurs into your product line could have been cost-effective.

NEW PRODUCTS

A careful examination of trends can often point the way to a new product. You may wish to develop a newsletter covering health, family, or environmental issues. The desire for family closeness has brought back an interest in board games. Perhaps you can develop a new card game. If you have a restaurant, you may meet the new market demand by creating take out "home-cooked" meals. Inventors Shows enable inventors and manufacturers to get together to put new products on the market. The U.S. Department of Commerce has listings of products for which foreign manufacturers' are seeking U.S. companies who will manufacture and sell these products to the U.S. market.

NEW SERVICES

Just as analysis of trends can indicate a market for new products, a need for new services will also be evident. With the popularity of the Cabbage Patch Doll, many dry cleaning establishments anticipated the need for cleaning these "well-loved" dolls and provided this service. Many desktop publishing and word processing services are being operated as home-based businesses. This equipment will need service and repair. Perhaps you could develop a mobile repair business for computer equipment.

Again, trade associations and publications can alert you to new services. Look for new products and equipment which will need future service and repair.

Remember that marketing is dynamic; your customers' likes and dislikes are constantly shifting. Be alert for the changing market.

RESOURCES: SURVEY THE MARKET

Husch, Tony and Linda Foust, **That's A Great Idea**, Gravity Publishing, Oakland, CA 1986.

U.S. SMALL BUSINESS ADMINISTRATION
P. O. Box 30
Denver, CO 80201-0030

"Finding a New Product for Your Company"
Management Aid 2.006
"Can You Make Money with Your Idea or Invention"
Management Aid 2.013
"Ideas Into Dollars"
Small Business Bibliography 91

U.S. DEPARTMENT OF COMMERCE
Contact the local field office listed in phone directory

"Licensing Opportunities Section" of the International Commerce Magazine. Lists foreign products available for licensing for sale and manufacture in the U.S.

OFFICE OF INVENTIONS AND INNOVATIONS
National Bureau of Standards
Washington, DC 20234

Request a listing of the major inventor's shows throughout the U.S.

NATIONAL TRADE AND PROFESSIONAL ASSOCIATIONS OF THE U.S.
Reference book published by Columbia Books
Washington, D.C.

2

PROTECTING YOUR IDEA

Disclosure letter

Journal

Copyright

Trademark

Patents

2 PROTECTING YOUR IDEA

When you are developing your product or service, you want to make certain that you are not infringing on the rights of others. You also want to get protection for your own work. Don't let the fear of having your idea stolen keep you from the marketplace. In order to develop and sell ideas, you have to disclose them.

This is a good time to discuss the safeguards of a disclosure letter and a journal and the protections under the federal law of copyright, trademark, and patent.

DISCLOSURE LETTER

One way to protect your idea is through the use of a disclosure letter. This is a letter outlining your idea for your new product or service, detailing the research and work you have done to date, and citing the people you have contacted while doing your research. Date the letter and have it notarized. The purpose of the disclosure letter is to verify the date on which the idea was yours. File the letter in a safe place.

JOURNAL

Establishing a date by means of a disclosure letter is not enough. You must be able to demonstrate that you are involved in an **active business**, as opposed to a **passive business** activity. An active business is able to show continuous work and progress in developing the idea into a viable product or service. This may be done by keeping a **log** or **journal**. This is a diary which will show daily entries which will verify ongoing work. To be considered a legal document, the log must be a bound book (not loose-leaf), have consecutively numbered pages, be written in ink, and contain no erasures. If you make an error, line through it and make the correction. Include information regarding the people to whom you have spoken about your idea and the dates and locations of the meetings. The journal and the disclosure letter give you the security you need to begin your market research. You may be able to get further protection through copyright, trademark, or patent.

COPYRIGHT

The copyright law grants protection to authors of literary, dramatic, musical, and artistic works. The owner of a copyright is granted sole rights to print and reprint, and perform the work. Work created after 1978 is protected for the life of the author plus 50 years after his death. Three steps must be taken to secure a copyright:

PRODUCE THE WORK WITH A COPYRIGHT NOTICE

The rights to a work may be permanently lost unless all copies bear the copyright notice in the proper form. The notice must be securely affixed to the work where it can easily be seen.

PUBLISH THE WORK

In most cases, you cannot complete the registration filing process until you have shown or sold at least one item to the public.

REGISTER YOUR CLAIM WITH THE COPYRIGHT OFFICE

As soon as possible, after publication, you must send the following material to the copyright office:

a. **Application for Registration** - The appropriate form can be requested from the Copyright Office. You do not need professional help in filling out the form. It is very straightforward.
b. **Copies** - Send two copies of the best edition of the work as published. The "best edition" criteria is spelled out in the Copyright Office brochure dealing with your product's classification.
c. **Fees** - The registration fee for published works is $10.00.

Send the registration form, the requested copies, and the fee in the same envelope or package to the Registrar of Copyrights. Copyright registration becomes effective on the date of receipt by the Copyright Office if all the required elements are in acceptable form.

The **copyright notice** must follow a set format. To arrange the notice in any other manner could make it invalid. The copyright notice should consist of the following three elements:

1. The word **Copyright**, the abbreviation **Copr.**, or the symbol ©.
2. The **year date** of publication. This is ordinarily the year in which copies are first placed on sale.
3. The **name** of the copyright owner or owners.

The three elements described above must appear together on all copies of the work in the following form: © 1988 Jane Doe.

The Copyright Office will provide you with forms appropriate to your work. Their address has been listed at the end of this section.

TRADEMARK

A trademark is a word, symbol, or device used in connection with merchandise and pointing distinctly to the origin and ownership of the article to which it is applied. The strongest trademarks are the least complex.

You cannot trademark names or phrases in the public domain. Your mark must be unique. When you have decided on a mark, do some research to see that no one else is using it. Trademark directories are available in the library. If your trademark is clear, begin applying it to your goods. A trademark is established through use. You cannot complete the registration process for a trademark until your mark has been used in interstate trade at least once.

Application and filing information are available from the Patent and Trademark Office in Washington, D.C. Three steps must be followed in order to file:

1. **Application for Trademark** - The form is straight-forward and relatively easy to complete.
2. **Fee** - The registration fee for filing for a trademark is $200.00.
3. **Copies** - Send five specimens showing the mark as it is actually used. If the specimens are three-dimensional, photographs may be used.

There is a standard format for the use of the trademark symbol. The letters **TM** must be placed after **every** use of the trademark or symbol. This indicates that you have claimed that mark.

PATENTS

When you get an idea for a new invention or process, analyze the idea for originality and patentability. One of the most difficult and crucial steps to securing a patent is the determination of **novelty**. Establishing novelty involves two things.

1. Analyzing the device according to specific standards set down by the Trademark Office.
2. Seeing whether or not anyone else has patented it first.

The only sure way to do this is to conduct a search of Patent Office files. To help make these files available to the public, the Federal Government established the **Depository Library Program**. These libraries offer the publications of the U.S. Patent Classification System, contain current issues of U.S. Patents, maintain collections of earlier issued patents, and provide technical staff assistance in their use. A listing of Depositories is available through the Government Printing Office.

A search of patents can be informative. Besides indicating if your device is patentable, it may disclose patents better than yours, but not in production. You may be able to contact the inventor and arrange to have it manufactured and sold by your company.

Protecting Your Idea

The advantages of obtaining a patent are obvious. You must also realize that a number of obstacles may lie in your path. One of these obstacles is **interference**. This occurs when two or more applicants have applications pending for substantially the same invention. Another obstacle is **infringement** which occurs through the unauthorized manufacture, use, or sale of a patented item.

Another service provided for inventors by the Patent Office is the acceptance and preservation for a two-year period of papers disclosing an invention. This **disclosure document** is accepted as evidence of the dates of conception of the invention. It will be retained for two years. During that time you must show continuous work and demonstrate that you are involved in an active process. This can be accomplished through the use of a journal which was discussed earlier in this chapter.

SUMMARY

Once you have written, notarized, and filed your disclosure letter, have started your journal, and have explored the possibilities of copyright, trademark, and patent, you can begin to disclose your idea to the public. You may begin your market research with questionnaires and test marketing which will be discussed in the following chapters.

RESOURCES: PROTECTING YOUR IDEA

Husch, Tony and Linda Foust, **That's A Great Idea**, Gravity Press, Oakland, 1986.

COPYRIGHT OFFICE
Information and Publications Section, LM-455
Library of Congress
Washington, D.C. 20559

                Publications: 1. Catalogue of materials published
                                   2. Highlights of the New Copyright Law (#R99)
                                   3. Copyright Basics (R1)
                                   4. Trademarks (#R13)

PATENT & TRADEMARK OFFICE
U.S. Department of Commerce
Washington, D.C. 20231

                Note: Write and ask for catalogue of publications.

SUPERINTENDENT OF DOCUMENTS
U.S. Government Printing Office
Washington, D.C. 20402

        Write For: 1. General information concerning patents
                            2. General information concerning trademarks
                            3. Directory of U.S. Depository Libraries

U.S. SMALL BUSINESS ADMINISTRATION
1441 L. Street, N.W.
Washington, D.C. 20616

        Write for: 1. Introduction to Patents #MA 6.005
                            2. New Product Development #90

3

THE USE OF QUESTIONNAIRES

Format

Types of Information

Distribution

Evaluation of Response

3 THE USE OF QUESTIONNAIRES

Because marketing is a dynamic process, you must find a cost-effective method of keeping up with the changes occurring within the market. A previous section helped you identify products and services which are compatible with current trends. You now want to get a response from the market regarding the product or service you are interested in providing. Before you invest time and money in developing your idea, it is wise to determine if a need or desire for it exists in the buying community. Surveys are an excellent means of determining the response to what you have to offer. A questionnaire is the most common means of collecting data.

FORMAT

In formulating a questionnaire, you want to carefully choose the question structure, the wording, and the sequence. Determine what it is you need to know and then choose your questions. Wording is very important. Use simple, unbiased, and direct wording. Be aware of the sequence of your questions. The first question should generate interest.

A questionnaire begins with an introduction. Your initial contact with the reader is established in the opening statement. Tell just enough about the nature of your survey to arouse interest. Establish that you value the reader's response. We all like to feel that our opinions are important.

Next, you will begin work on the body of the questionnaire. Begin by making a list of the information you need. Don't worry about phrasing or order. Get everything down on paper, then go back and develop your wording and sequence. There are three types of questions and they vary according to structure and response.

OPEN-ENDED QUESTIONS

This type of question requires the respondent to provide the reply. He is not given choices; he must fill in the blanks.

MULTIPLE-CHOICE QUESTIONS

You provide the respondent with a selection of answers. One example would be yes or no type questions. There are only two responses. There is little chance of a biased answer. Some questions will warrant more choices. When using multiple choice questions, run different copies of the questionnaire and vary the order in which the choices appear following the question. People tend to select an answer from the front of the list and your results may be biased. If the question requires the respondent to choose an answer from a numerical list, there is a tendency to select an answer from the middle of the list. People wish to appear "average" or "normal," and assume that choices at either end of the range reflect extremes.

RATING QUESTIONS

These are sometimes called value-judgement questions. The respondent is asked to reflect his opinion on a ranking scale; for example, a scale of 1 to 10.

Try to phrase your questions so they are clear and easily understood. Choose language that is appropriate to the group who will be responding. Use terms that are familiar to the consumer. Avoid words or phrases which are unique to your industry and not in common usage.

Ask questions in a psychological sequence. Questions in a subject area should be grouped together. One question should logically follow another. The first question creates interest. Begin with general questions and build to the more specific. Ask the most difficult or involved questions at the end. They will be turn-offs if they appear early in the questionnaire. Since the respondent has completed most of the work by the time he gets to the more involved questions, he will be less apt to abandon the project.

The questionnaire ends with the "basic data:" the name, address, and phone number of the respondent. Often a more honest and objective response will result if providing this information is optional. Many questionnaire respondents prefer to remain anonymous.

TYPES OF INFORMATION

A well-designed questionnaire can gather data covering four main areas: interest in your product or service, demographics, competition, and the means of reaching the market.

QUESTIONS AIMED AT DETERMINING A NEED FOR YOUR PRODUCT OR SERVICE.

1. Do you like to play card and/or board games?
2. Do you own a personal computer?
3. In the past two months, how many times have you eaten take-out food?
4. Would you be interested in take-out, "home-cooked" food?
5. Do you have an interest in environmental health issues?

QUESTIONS WHICH SHOW YOU THE KIND OF PEOPLE YOUR PROSPECTS ARE.

1. Do you work away from your home city?
2. Do you shop where you work?
3. Do you shop where you live?
4. Would you be interested in home delivery or in-home service during evening or weekend hours?
5. Into which of these age groups do you fall?
6. What is your occupation?
7. Do you own or rent your home?
8. What is your household income?

QUESTIONS WHICH SHOW YOU HOW TO REACH THE RESPONDENTS.

1. What newspapers do you read?
2. What section do you read first?
3. What radio stations do you listen to?
4. What TV programs do you regularly watch?
5. Which magazines do you read?
6. Do you use discount coupons?
7. In the last 6 months, how many times did you order a product from a catalog?

QUESTIONS ABOUT THE COMPETITION.

1. What company do you currently use?
2. Are you satisfied with their service?
3. How could service be improved to meet your needs?
4. What take-out food do you eat?
5. Are you satisfied?
6. If not, how could it be improved?

These example questions are in a simple format to give you an idea of the type of information you can gather in each category. Refer to the previous section format when structuring your own questions. References have been listed at the end of this chapter which can give you additional information and examples.

DISTRIBUTION

Decide who is to be surveyed, how many people are to be contacted, and how they will be reached. They can be contacted by mail, telephone, personal or group interview.

For a questionnaire's results to be valid, it must have been distributed to potential customers. Don't give it out to friends and family and expect results which will reflect those of your market.

DIRECT MAIL:

Unfortunately, the mail as a market research vehicle has been overused and you must extend some courtesies to increase your response rate. Include a self-addressed, stamped envelope in all your mailings to encourage the recipient to return the questionnaire. Offer discount coupons. Some entrepreneurs are increasing the response rate by enclosing a dollar bill in each mailing accompanied by a note thanking the respondent for taking the time to complete the form. There is a moral obligation to respond! Hand address the envelopes. This takes time, but has proven to increase the response rate. Metered mail is a turn-off; use stamps for a personalized impression.

Carefully choose your sampling group. This can most effectively be done by renting a mailing list from a list broker (look under "Mailing Lists" in the Yellow Pages). Note that you will **rent** the list. Mailing lists are rented for a one-time use. A small percentage of the names on your list will be those of list company employees. They will log in your mailing. If a second piece of literature is received from you, a check will be made to see if you have rented for a second mailing. If you are reusing a one-time rental, you may be denied future rentals. Anyone who responds to your mailing becomes your customer and you can send out repeat mailings to them. The company employees do not respond to offers.

Your study of trends and your ultimate choice of a product or service to research will have given some clues as to prospective customers. The broker can prepare a list according to the information you give regarding age, occupation, sex, buying habits, education, interests, family status, income, and geographic location. Get a feeling for who you think will be interested, rent a list, send out your questionnaire, and see if the results agree with your original assessment.

The more specific and narrow you make your list, the more you will pay per name. You will pay more for a list targeting high income professionals who live in Beverly Hills, eat out three or more times per week, are married with no children, and own BMWs than for a list of high income, married residents of Beverly Hills. A more specific list could be more cost-effective in the long run if it helps you clearly define your market.

TELEMARKETING:

Telephone surveys are another means of gathering data. This medium is also being overused; consumers are increasingly unwilling to take calls from strangers who are conducting surveys.

You may wish to have the survey done for you by a telemarketing survey company. Research firms have specially trained people who may have more success in getting a response. Even if you have an outside agency conduct the study, you can still make recommendations regarding the questions asked.

If you decide to do your own telemarketing survey, make use of your original questionnaire. Prepare a good introduction: "I am calling a few people in your neighborhood for an important and quick survey. I hope you will take a moment to tell me how you feel about ____." Then refer to your questionnaire to gather the information you need. The phone company can provide a directory of geographical listings so you can target any area.

PERSONAL INTERVIEWS:
Some shopping centers and malls will allow you to canvass shoppers. Be sure to check with the center's management regarding their policy. Dress in a business-like manner and carry a clipboard to hold your questionnaires. Talking to shoppers can be a valuable learning experience. Be aware of shopping patterns. The market segment you interview on Tuesday morning will be quite different from the segment represented by Saturday afternoon shoppers.

You may be able to set up a display table at a fair or art show. Have some folding chairs available so you can conduct interviews and get questionnaire responses.

You may wish to hire interviewers to do the work for you. You can hire students, temporary help from agencies, or professional interviewers listed in the yellow pages.

GROUP INTERVIEWS:
Contact local clubs and organizations to see if you can make a presentation on your new product or service. You can offer a donation to the group's treasury in return for the opportunity to present your case. A group discussion may give you some insight into potential problem areas. Hand out your questionnaires or present the questions for discussion. Be aware of the types of people present. Clubs are usually composed of people with similar likes. There may be a dominant person who is capable of swaying the others. Your results may be biased, but the experience will still provide valuable information.

You may choose to hire a marketing research firm which will have interviewers on staff. They will be listed in the yellow pages.

EVALUATION OF THE RESPONSE

Plan your strategy for evaluation while you are developing your questionnaire. Use an **address code** on all mailings. For example, if your mailing address is 216 Main Street, code your return address by adding Suite 206 or Dept. 688. Suite 206 could be the code for mailings sent to a specific area. If the questionnaires are returned unsigned, you will still be able to have an idea of the geographical area responding. Department 688 could refer to a mailing sent in June of 1988. Use as many codes as you feel you need. You may color code your mailings. Print your questionnaires on different colors or different types of paper. Again, you will have a clear picture of the response from an area.

Use the same basic questionnaire in your research for comparable results. Then you can form a composite from your telephone, personal, and group interviews and your questionnaire results.

When you have compiled the data, view it objectively. Because marketing is a dynamic process, you must be flexible regarding your results. Perhaps your original product or service idea wasn't well received. Did the survey point the way to a modification of your idea which would better serve your market?

A sample **questionnaire**, a **coding log**, and a **marketing research worksheet** follow this section.

RESOURCES: QUESTIONNAIRES

Breen, George and A. B. Blankership, **Do-it-Yourself Market Research**, McGraw-Hill, N.Y., 1982.

Erdos, **Professional Mail Surveys**, McGraw-Hill, N.Y., 1970.

(resources on preparing and using questionnaires)

DIRECT MAIL/MARKETING ASSOCIATION
6 E. 43rd Street
New York, NY 10017

(information on direct mail and mailing lists)

SAMPLE QUESTIONNAIRE FOR A PRODUCT

I am developing a new product and am contacting a few people in your neighborhood for an important and quick survey. I hope you will take a moment to tell me how you feel about board games.

1. Do you play any board games? ____Yes ____No
   (If NO, please go to #7)

2. What is your favorite board game?
   (Only one answer)

   ____Backgammon ____Checkers ____Pictionary ____Life
   ____Clue ____Monopoly ____Sorry ____Other

3. On the average, how often do your play board games?
   (If conducting phone or personal interview, insert name of game stated in question #2)

   ____Less than once per month ____Once per month
   ____Twice per month ____Once per week
   ____More than once per week

4. Would you consider playing a new board game about the Stock Market?
   ____Yes ____No ____Maybe ____I don't know

5. How much would you pay for a board game about the stock market?
   ____$6.00 to $10.00 ____$10.01 to $15.00 ____$15.01 to $20.00
   ____Over $20.00

6. What is the first word that comes to mind when you think of the Stock Market?
   _____

7. On the average, how many hours of television do you watch per week?
   ____Less than one hour ____1 to 3 hours ____$3\frac{1}{2}$ to 6 hours
   ____$6\frac{1}{2}$ to 9 hours ____$9\frac{1}{2}$ hours or more

8. Do you clip coupons from the newspaper? ____Yes ____No

9. What radio station do you listen to most often? _____

10. What is your age?
    ____18 to 24 years ____25 to 34 years ____35 to 44 years
    ____45 to 54 years ____55 + Years

11. What is your sex? ____Male ____Female

12. What is your average household income?
    ____Under $10,000 ____$10,001-20,000 ____$20,001-30,000
    ____$30,001-40,000 ____$40,001-50,000 ____$50,001-75,000
    ____Over $75,000

Thank you for your response. The following information is helpful to my study, but is optional:

Name_____

Address_____

City_____ State_____ Zip Code_____

(Questionnaire prepared by Suzanne J. Wong)

SAMPLE QUESTIONNAIRE
FOR A SERVICE

I am developing a new service and am contacting a few people in your neighborhood for an important and quick survey. I hope you will take a moment to tell me how you feel about take-out food.

1. Do you order take-out food? ____Yes ____No
   (If NO, please go to #9)

2. What is your favorite take-out food?
   (Only one answer)
   ____Chinese food ____Mexican food ____Pizza ____Deli food
   ____Burgers ____Other

3. On the average, how often do you order take-out food?
   (If conducting phone or personal interview, insert name of food stated in #2)
   ____Less than once per month ____Once per month
   ____Twice per month ____Once per week
   ____More than once per week

4. Would you be interested in full course take-out meals? ____Yes ____No

5. Would you be interested in home delivered meals? ____Yes ____No

6. How much would you be willing to pay for a full course, home-delivered meal?
   ____$5.00 ____$7.50 ____$10.00 ____$12.00

7. What is the first word that comes into your mind when you think of full course, home-delivered meals?

   _____

8. On a scale of 1 to 5, with 5 signifying very important, please rank the following items as they relate to your feelings about take-out food:

   Containers.................... 1 2 3 4 5   (please circle answer)
   Combinations of foods offered... 1 2 3 4 5
   Temperature when served.......... 1 2 3 4 5
   Taste......................... 1 2 3 4 5
   Delivery time................. 1 2 3 4 5

9. On the average, how many hours of television do you watch per week?
   ____Less than one hour ____1 to 3 hours ____3½ to 6 hours
   ____6½ to 9 hours ____9½ hours or more

10. Do you clip coupons from the newspaper? ____Yes ____No

11. What newspaper do your read? _____

12. What radio station do you listen to most often? _____

13. What is your age:
    ____18 to 24 years ____25 to 34 years ____35 to 44 years
    ____45 to 54 years ____55+ years

14. What is your sex? ____Male ____Female

15. What is your average household income?
    ____Under $10,000 ____$10,000 - 20,001 ____$20,001 - 30,000
    ____$30,001 - 40,000 ____$40,001 - 50,000 ____$50,001 to 75,000
    ____Over $75,000

Thank you for your response. The following information is helpful to my study, but is optional:

Name_____

Address_____

City_____State_____Zip_____

QUESTIONNAIRE CODING LOG

CODE	DATE	NO. SENT	DESTINATION/RECIPIENT	RESPONSE RATE	EVALUATION

QUESTIONS	INFORMATION SOURCE	RESULTS	EFFECT ON PLAN

MARKETING RESEARCH WORKSHEET

4

TESTING THE MARKET

Prototype

Testing a Product

Testing a Service

Letters of Reference

4 TESTING THE MARKET

If your questionnaire results have indicated a positive response to your new idea, you will want to proceed with some test marketing of your new product or service. It's much more reliable to judge a potential customer's reaction to a product or service by observing his reaction to an actual sample of your work.

The results of your telephone, personal, and group interviews and your questionnaire responses should have defined a group interested in what you have to offer. Go back to that group for your test marketing.

PROTOTYPE

Make up a sample of your product. This **prototype** will enable you to analyze the cost involved in manufacturing the item. You will see the time and energy needed for production. You may get an indication of design or material changes which can reduce costs. The prototype is the link between your idea and the final version. It is the refining stage.

Your prototype will depend upon the nature of your product. There are three prototype catagories:

1. **Mock-up** - A mock-up is a nonfunctional representation of your product intended to show basic design, size, and color in a three-dimensional form. Since you want to demonstrate the final product, a nonfunctional mock-up will not be adequate for mechanical projects.
2. **Working model** - A working model is made from different materials but is completely functional. It can be handled and can be used in demonstrations.
3. **Production model** - A production model is made of the same materials, is the same size, and performs the same function as the final product.

Depending upon your time, talent, financial resources, and the complexity of the project, you can produce the prototype yourself or pay someone else to make it.

Companies specializing in this service can be found listed in the Yellow Pages under: "Designers-Industrial" or "Designers-Product." College Industrial Design Departments may also be of assistance in building functioning models. A prototype is essential to the market research of a product.

TESTING A PRODUCT

You are ready to take your idea, in the form of a prototype or the actual product, into the real world. There are advertising agencies and market research firms who will conduct studies for you. The entrepreneur may find these services too costly. You may choose to do your own test marketing.

Your research targeted a certain group as potential buyers of your product. Approach that group with "the real thing." Allow them to use the item and ask them questions. Negative responses can work for you. How can the product be changed to make it more acceptable? Try different types of packaging. Feedback will give you insight into your final packaging design.

For example, if you are developing a newsletter on environmental issues, print the newsletter on a few different colors and types of paper. Change the format and type style. Get feedback from your group regarding readability and acceptance, as well as content. If you have developed a new board or card game, gather a group to play the game. Are your rules too complicated or not clear? Print the game using different colors and materials and see which are most acceptable. If you are testing take-out, "home-cooked" foods, experiment with packaging. Do consumers prefer styrofoam or cardboard containers? What combinations of foods are most acceptable?

Contact service organizations and clubs about the possibility of presenting a group participation program on what you are offering. Discuss your newsletter and hand out samples, present your game and have the group play a few rounds, or provide your take-out, "home-cooked" foods as the menu for the group's next luncheon or dinner meeting. Be sure to have evaluation sheets prepared and available to get written as well as verbal responses.

TESTING A SERVICE

In order to test a service, you will have to provide that service and then evaluate the response. Approach your targeted group. If you are starting a house-cleaning service, offer four hours of service in return for an evaluation and a letter of recommendation. If you will be adding home delivery to your "home-cooked" food line, provide some complimentary meals. Ask the recipients if the temperature, food variety, and taste were acceptable. Look for feedback which will help you develop your service into one which will be well received by your customers.

LETTERS OF REFERENCE

When using endorsements or testimonials from customers, you must be sure to follow the guidelines set forth by the Federal Trade Commission regarding truth in advertising. Endorsements and testimonials must be based on actual use of the product or service. You may be required by the FTC to submit evidence to substantiate the claims.

In order to be valid, a letter of reference or endorsement must be prepared by the actual consumer and must contain a clause giving you permission to use the statements in your advertising and promotion. Keep these letters on file and be prepared to produce them if asked to verify your claims.

While studying trends, developing and protecting your idea, and evaluating your test marketing responses, you have become aware of the competition. The next chapter will give you insights regarding evaluation of the competition.

RESOURCES: MARKET TESTING

U.S. SMALL BUSINESS ADMINISTRATION
P. O. Box 30
Denver, CO 80201-0030

"Tips for Getting More for Your Marketing Dollar"
Management Aid 4.008
"Learning About Your Market"
Management Aid 4.019
"Marketing Research Procedures"
Small Business Bibliography 9

FEDERAL TRADE COMMISSION
Pennsylvania Avenue and 6th Street N.W.
Washington, DC 20580

"Advertising, Packaging, and Labeling"

Levinson, Jay, **Guerrilla Marketing**, Houghton, Mifflin, Boston, 1984

EVALUATING THE COMPETITION

Finding the Competition

Evaluating the Competitive Service

Evaluating the Competitive Product

Uniqueness and Benefit to the Customer

5 EVALUATING THE COMPETITION

Direct competition will be a business offering the same product or service to the same market. **Indirect competition** is a company with the same product or service but a different market. You may both be manufacturing the same item, but the other company is offering the product for sale through mail order while yours will be available through a retail outlet. Your service may be provided through a mobile unit while the competition provides the same service in his shop. Evaluate both direct and indirect competition.

In a retail business, the toughest competition generally comes from established stores and wholesalers who can offer lower prices because of higher sales volume. In the service industry, strong competition comes from established businesses that have a loyal clientele. Examine the extent and nature of the competition in terms of location, product or service, pricing, methods of distribution, packaging, and source of supply.

Look for the strengths and weaknesses of your competitors. You need to identify your competitor's image. To what part of the market does he appeal? Can you appeal to that same market in a better way? Or can you discover an untapped market?

FINDING THE COMPETITION

If your original questionnaire contained questions regarding current service businesses and products used by your market, you will have a head start. Perhaps your individual and group interviews gave you some insight.

The Yellow Pages of the telephone directory can provide a wide variety of useful information. The total listing in your business category will give you an idea of the range of your competition. You will be able to pinpoint their locations within your geographical area. Analyze the type and style of the ad itself. What image do you have of the business based solely on your reaction to their ad? When you make an inspection trip to the place of business, do you retain that same image?

The Chamber of Commerce can give you a wealth of information on business, in general, and your business area, in particular, for the region you wish to investigate.

National Trade and Professional Associations publish newsletters and magazines which not only predict trends, but also tell about current business. A directory available in the library lists all the associations. Identify those in your field, write them on your letterhead, and request sample copies of their publications and membership information.

When you have compiled a list of competitors, plan to visit each one. Make copies of the **Competition Evaluation Form** at the end of this chapter. Use them to help you gather the data you need.

EVALUATING THE COMPETITIVE SERVICE

The most effective way to evaluate a competitive service is to pose as a customer. Call and ask for job rates, delivery schedules, terms of payment, discount policies, and warranties or guarantees. For example, if you are starting a house cleaning service, find out the minimum number of hours for which you can hire the service? If the minimum service is 4 hours, is there a market among apartment and condominium dwellers for a weekly 2 hour service? Does the homeowner supply cleaning materials? Would your customers appreciate your providing and using a high powered commercial vacuum? If you are pursuing the idea of home delivery of take-out foods, how do existing businesses handle this? How much time passes between order receipt and delivery?

What was your overall reaction after the call? Do you have confidence in the company? Were you treated in a courteous manner? Were you put on hold and forced to listen to inane music or a series of ads? Your reactions will reflect those of the buying public.

Visit your competitor's place of business. Rate the personnel. Is service prompt and efficient? A collegue who was interested in opening a dry cleaning establishment, parked outside one competitor's shop at 7:30 a.m. The shop was due to open at 8:00 a.m. During that time prior to opening, seven customers arrived only to find the business closed. The entrepreneur saw a need for opening his dry cleaners at 7:30 a.m. to reach that segment of the market which was being overlooked. Park outside the take-out food establishment we mentioned earlier. When are the peak ordering times? How many drivers are needed? You will get an idea of the volume of business.

Now make use of the competitor's service. Was the housecleaning acceptable? What could be improved? Order the take-out food. Was it delivered in the estimated time frame and was it still hot?

Your analysis of this wealth of information on the competition will help you plan your own market entry.

EVALUATING A COMPETITIVE PRODUCT

Visit shops where products similar to yours are displayed. Are the personnel knowledgeable? In our board or card game example, visit a game store. Ask a sales clerk to explain a game similar to yours. If the explanation isn't good enough to encourage you to buy the merchandise, you may decide to put a good, thorough description on the game box. Your own packaging may be what will sell the merchandise, not the sales clerk. How are the games displayed and what are their price ranges? Visit the shop at different times on different days of the week. You will begin to get an idea of traffic flow patterns. Watch the displays of similar products. Do the products seem to be moving? How soon are they marked down or moved to the sale table? Most stores

keystone or double the wholesale cost, so you can get an estimate of what your competitors' wholesale prices may be.

We've referred to the environmental newsletter in our examples. Request samples of similar newsletters. Examine type styles, paper quality, and content. How often are they published? Do they include ads to help offset publishing costs?

Gather data and draw your conclusions about the competition.

UNIQUENESS AND BENEFIT TO THE CUSTOMER

You will bring the strengths of the competition to your business and you will learn from their weaknesses. The weaknesses are your inroads to success. They point the way toward what will be **unique** about your business. They will help you target what will **benefit the customer.**

The entrepreneur who observed the seven customers who were turned away from the dry cleaning establishment between 7:30 and 8:00 found a way to be unique. He will benefit his customers by opening at 7:30 a.m.

The game maker discovered a need for a clear explanation on the cover of the game box. The customer is benefited by knowing the basic idea of the game and the skill level.

A tree trimmer in San Francisco advertises that he "puts down mats to protect your sod." We get a mental image of a tree surgeon who cares about our lawn and won't allow falling limbs to gouge holes in it. It doesn't matter that most of these businesses provide this service. He is capitalizing on it to make his mat placement unique and a benefit to his customers.

Analyze advertising with a critical eye and you will begin to see a pattern. We all use shampoo to get our hair clean, but no shampoo company advertises that their product will get your hair "clean." It will get your hair "cleaner," make it "more manageable," or has a "fresher scent." Find what is unique about your product or service and how that uniqueness will benefit the customer. This uniqueness will be stressed to develop your identity and to prepare you to take on the competition.

Your new product or service may be a monopoly. If successful, you can be certain that competition will follow. You will evaluate the competition throughout the lifetime of your business. To remain competitive, you may have to adjust your pricing schedule, redesign your packaging, or change your advertising.

RESOURCES: EVALUATING THE COMPETITION

SMALL BUSINESS ADMINISTRATION

    "Creative Selling - The Competitive Edge"
    Management Aid 4.002

COMPETITION EVALUATION WORKSHEET

1. NAME OF COMPETITOR:

2. LOCATION:

3. PRODUCT:

4. SERVICE:

5. PACKAGING:

6. PRICE:

7. METHODS OF DISTRIBUTION:

8. SUPPLIERS:

9. STRENGTHS:

10. WEAKNESSES:

11. ADDITIONAL INFORMATION:

NOTE: A Competition Evaluation Worksheet should be made for each competitor. Keep these resords and update them. It pays to continue to rate your competition.

6

FINDING YOUR TARGET MARKET

Demographics

Psychographics

Putting it Together

6 FINDING YOUR TARGET MARKET

Now that you have determined that there is a need for what you have to offer and have analyzed the competition in terms of how they are filling that need, you are ready to define your **target market** (your customers). You are going to identify the market segment you can serve profitably based on market size, resources needed, and your strengths and weaknesses. You don't want to become too big, too soon and not be able to meet deadlines and production schedules. Your goal is to develop a profile of your customers. This profile is formed based on demographic and psychographic information.

DEMOGRAPHICS

Markets are described in terms of demographics: age, sex, ethnic background, education, occupation, income, family status, and geographic location. Based upon your observations while analyzing the competition and your results from questionnaire evaluation, you have developed a profile of your customers. You now want to find more customers who will fit this profile.

The information you need is available in Census Reports published by the Department of Commerce, in directories available in the Reference Section of the library, and in data available through the Chambers of Commerce.

Population size is one of several factors you will use to help you determine the size of the market. A study of population tables in the **Statistical Abstract of the United States** (reference material published by the Department of Commerce) will show population shifts. When studied, trends begin to emerge.

There is a shift of the more affluent city dwellers to suburban communities. This requires an adjustment on the part of business. Where does your market live? Where do they work? Do they shop where they live or where they work? If your potential customers shop where they work and work in another city, it will do no good to offer your product or service to them during normal working hours in the city of their residence.

The major **population** areas of the Middle Atlantic and the East-North Central Regions are continuing to grow. Population is expanding in the Mountain and Pacific areas. The Sun Belt area is a region of rapid growth, primarily because of the increased number of retirees. Trends indicate a movement away from farms and to urban areas.

It is also useful to know the trends in **age distribution**. In the mid-1980's, the number of people age 65 and over surpassed the number of teenagers. This gap will widen as we move into the 1990's. The response by business to this trend is substantial. Ads feature models over 50, movies and television programs deal with subjects of interest to the older segment of the population, and new products have hit the market. There is a marked contrast to the youth-oriented promotions of the last decade.

Sex is an obvious basis for consumer market analysis. Many of the traditional buying patterns are changing. Men are frequent food shoppers, women are buying gas and arranging for car repair, and both are now concerned with home maintenance.

The number of working women has risen considerably in all age groups. In the late 1980's well over one half of all American women were working outside the home. By 1990, women will constitute almost one half of the U.S. labor force.

For some products and services, it is useful to analyze the population based on **ethnic origin**. Product preferences, age distribution, population shifts, and language will vary. You should be aware of the ethnic breakdown of the geographical area you are targeting. This data is found in the Census Bureau information dealing with general population characteristics.

Education level points to changes in product preference. People with higher levels of education generally have more specialized tastes and higher incomes.

Occupation must also be considered as a meaningful criterion for analyzing the market. Young executives may earn the same income as auto mechanics. The different attitudes, experiences, and other life-style factors of the two groups will lead to different buying patterns.

Family status must be analyzed. During the past decade, two distinct and new groups have emerged: single people living alone and unmarried people living together. Census reports break down family status by number of children and their age ranges. Data will indicate single parent homes, retirees, and marital status. If your target market falls into one of these groups, census data will help you locate them.

Income is another important consideration. A market requires more than people; it requires money. A knowledge of income, its distribution, and how it is spent is essential if you are to know your market.

Over the past years, there has been a tremendous growth in middle and upper income markets. This trend is expected to continue. Some of this growth is attributed to dual-income families. Regional income data will help pinpoint your market. Income data on cities will be helpful in choosing your location. Much of this information is available through your local Chamber of Commerce. The trend toward higher income increases the amount of discretionary money available for spending in the marketplace. This will lead to increased demand for food, clothing, travel, and entertainment.

PSYCHOGRAPHICS

Psychographics are the psychological characteristics of your market and are as important a demographics. The traditional demographic studies gave no insight into why people bought certain products over those of the competition. Marketers began to see the need for analyzing lifestyle, personal behavior, self-concept, and buying style. The study of psychographics and its relationship to marketing is relatively new. It had its beginnings in the early 1950's. At the present time, it is a widely used tool for analyzing the market.

Lifestyle is a person's manner of living. It is a broad category and involves personality characteristics. Life-style relates to a customer's activities, interests, and opinions. It reflects how he spends his leisure time. Does he spend evenings at home or does he go out? Demographic studies may have identified the market, but if the majority of that market goes out to eat, your take-out food business will suffer.

Personal behavior is tied to personal values. The degree of community involvement, political activity, and neighborhood participation reflect the pychological makeup of a person. The degree of cautiousness, skepticism, and ambition reflects on buying patterns.

Self-concept is how a person sees himself and hopes to be seen by others. The demographics of family size, location, occupation, and income level may indicate that an individual would purchase a station wagon, but the psychographics of self-image show that he would buy a sports car.

The **buying style** of your market is critical. How often do they make a purchase? Was there a specific reason for the purchase or was it an impulse buy? New products are first purchased by individuals who perceive themselves as adventuresome and open-mined.

Your questionnaires can give you feedback regarding the psychographics of your group. Include questions to get the information you need.

PUTTING IT TOGETHER

The key to market research is gathering useful information: information that is timely and reliable. It is an orderly, objective way of learning about the people who will buy your product or use your service. A **Target Market Worksheet** has been included for your use in defining your market. A resource list follows this section to help you locate sources and gather the data you need. Your questionnaire results will form a basis for zeroing in on your customers.

Remember that marketing is a changing process. Customers move, lifestyles change, income levels vary. To work effectively, market research must occur continuously throughout the lifetime of your business. Always be alert for new competition, new products and services, population shifts, and new trends.

When you have identified your target market, you are ready to position your business and move into the marketplace. The next section, **REACHING YOUR TARGET MARKET**, will cover this area.

RESOURCES: FINDING YOUR TARGET MARKET

FEDERAL GOVERNMENT

1. Bureau of the Budget
   Standard Industrial Classification Manual: This publication lists the SIC numbers issued to major areas of business: for example, the SIC number for piano tuning is #7699.
   Standard Metropolitan Statistical Areas

2. Bureau of the Census
   Issues publications covering demographic and economic surveys.

3. Department of Commerce
   Census of Business: Retail Area Statistics
   Census Tract Manual
   County & City Data Book: This book is updated every three years and contains statistical information on population, education, employment, income, housing, and retail sale
   County Business Patterns
   Directory of Federal Statistics for Local Areas
   Facts for Marketers
   Measuring Markets: A guide to the use of federal and state statistical data.

4. Small Business Administration
   National Directories for Use in Marketing
   Small Marketers Aids
   Statistics and Maps for Market Analysis

STATE GOVERNMENT

1. State Department of Commerce
2. Office of the Secretary of State
3. State Bookstore

LOCAL GOVERNMENT

1. Regulatory Agencies
2. Urban and Redevelopment Agencies

NON-GOVERNMENT SOURCES

1. Banks
2. Chambers of Commerce
3. Community and State Colleges
4. Entrepreneurs (local business owners)
5. Merchant Associations
6. Retired Entrepreneurs (S.C.O.R.E. counselors may be contacted through the S.B.A.)
7. Suppliers and Wholesalers
8. Trade Associations (Clearing houses for information passing between industry, government, and the general public)

PRINTED MATERIAL

1. Directories which are compiled by Chambers of Commerce and Merchants Associations
2. Magazines and Journals
   Advertising Age
   Advertising and Sales Promotion
   Business Horizons
   Business Week
   Harvard Business Review
   Industrial Marketing
   Journal of Advertising Research
   Journal of Business
   Journal of Marketing
   Journal of Marketing Research
   Wall Street Journal
3. The Yellow Pages
4. Newspapers

LIBRARIES

Publications and Directories available in the Reference Section.

Business Periodicals Index: A monthly listing of business articles appearing in a wide variety of business publications.
Directory of Directories: Describes over 9,000 buyer's guides and directories.
Dun and Bradstreet Directories: List companies alphabetically, geographically, and by product classification.
Encyclopedia of Associations: Provides information on every major trade and professional association in the United States.
Marketing Information Guide: Provides a monthly annotated bibliography of marketing information.
Standard and Poor's Industry Surveys: Updated statistics and analyses of industries.
Statistical Abstract of the U.S.: Updated annually, provides demographic, economic, and social information.
U.S. Industrial Outlook: Provides projections of industrial activity.

TARGET MARKET WORKSHEET

WHO ARE MY CUSTOMERS?

1. PROFILE:

    Economic Level -

    Psychological Make-up -

    Age -

    Sex -

    Income Level -

    Buying Habits -

2. LOCATION:

    Live -

    Work -

    Shop -

3. MARKET SIZE:

4. COMPETITION:

5. OTHER FACTORS:

CUSTOMER NEEDS	WHAT CAN I OFFER?

Finding Your Target Market

PART II

REACHING YOUR TARGET MARKET

Positioning Your Product or Service

Pricing

Package Design

Methods of Distribution

Location

Timing of Market Entry

Advertising Your Business

7

POSITIONING YOUR PRODUCT OR SERVICE

7 POSITIONING YOUR PRODUCT OR SERVICE

Throughout your marketing experience, you will hear the term **positioning**. A product or service position is determined by its image projected in terms of the competition, pricing, packaging, distribution, location, and timing of market entry.

For some products, the best position is directly against the competition. This is evidenced when companies such as Pepsi-Cola and Coca-Cola develop new product lines. Both companies have a similar product line appealing to the same market.

If the competition is established and has a strong market position, you may want to use your position to establish uniqueness. Hertz was well established in the car rental businesss. Avis capitalized on being number 2 and trying harder.

Some stores are known for high quality merchandise and high prices. Others have the image of discount stores. Once position is established, it is very difficult to change that position in terms of price and quality. Discount stores have a hard time upgrading image through the introduction of higher quality merchandise at higher prices. By the same token, the introduction of discount products into a high-scale store would have a negative reaction. The move would cloud the company's image, confuse the customers, and probably reduce the store's share of the market.

Your market research will have given you insights into the ways in which to position your product. You know your competition, how they advertise, and who they serve. You have compared the pricing structures, the distribution channels, the packaging, and the locations of competitors. Positioning is much like a ranking system. Determine where you want to be on the ladder. The next chapters will give you information for refining your pricing, packaging, methods of distribution and deciding upon your location and timing of market entry as you get ready to enter the marketplace.

8

PRICING

8 PRICING

To be successful, the small business person must establish prices for goods and services that will appeal to the customer, will be competitive with similar businesses, and will allow for a profit margin. Pricing can "make or break" you. If your price is wrong, it won't matter if everything else is right.

There are four major elements to consider in setting a price:

1. How much does it cost to produce the product or to provide the service?
2. What are the operating expenses of the business?
3. How much profit do you want to make?
4. Will the customer buy it at that price?

Your first consideration will be to consider the **costs** to produce your product or provide your service. If you are manufacturing the product, you must take into account **all** the labor and materials that go into its production. If you are a retailer, the basic factor in determining the selling price of the product is the wholesale price of the product. Don't overlook shipping charges. To determine the total cost of merchandise, add the transportation charges to the supplier's price. The small business which provides a service has other considerations. Repair shops have to consider the cost of parts they use. Generally, their biggest expenses are salaries and equipment.

The **operating expenses** of your business are your overhead costs. They consist of all the overhead costs that are not directly related to the production of your goods or the performance of your service. The cost of raw materials and labor change in direct proportion to changes in production. Overhead remains constant. You will hear overhead or operating expenses referred to as **fixed expenses** and cost of goods purchased or service provided referred to as **direct expenses**.

A worksheet entitled **Cash to be Paid Out** has been provided to help you realize and record all the expenses which may be incurred by your business.

There is little in print to help you price new products. Generally, product makers have to rely on their own intuition and marketing knowledge to arrive at a good price. Two of the easiest formulas for determining pricing are shown on worksheets at the end of this chapter. The **Hourly Rate Formula** covers the means of arriving at an hourly rate to charge in a service industry and the **Formula for Manufacturers** covers a method for determining the wholesale price of a product.

Pricing

In her book, **HOMEMADE MONEY**, Barbara Brabec presents one of the easiest formulas for determining an hourly rate. It was originally formulated by Libby Platus and published in **THE CRAFTS REPORT**. The **hourly rate formula** can be used to determine how much to charge per hour if you are providing a service. You will need to determine your desired annual net income. How much profit would you like to have at the end of the year? Also figure out how many hours you want to work per year on the service you will provide. Be sure to include the hours spent on office work, errand running, and other miscellaneous business-related work. Now compute a figure for your annual expenses based on a total from your estimates on the amount of cash to be paid out.

The formula is the **desired annual net income** divided by the **number of hours worked per year**. This amount is added to the **annual expenses** divided by the **number of hours worked per year**. This formula will give you the hourly rate you must charge in order to realize your desired net income. Refer to the sample **Hourly Rate Formula Worksheet** at the end of this chapter. The following data has been used to compute the rate:

Desire annual net income = $10,000

Number of hours worked per year = 1,000
(20 hours per week x 50 weeks)

Annual expenses = $8,000
(from **Cash to be Paid Out Worksheets**)

In order to net $10,000 per year, you will have to work 1,000 hours per year and charge $18.00 per hour. This formula allows for flexibility. Do you want to make more profit? Then you can work more hours per year. If you do this, be sure to increase your annual expenses accordingly. If you work more hours, you will be increasing the use of utilities, consumable supplies, etc. A decrease in your annual expenses will decrease the rate per hour. This is to your advantage. You can still charge $18.00 per hour. The difference is a bonus! Perhaps $18.00 is too much to charge based on your competition. Lower your annual net income, lower your annual expenses, or work more hours. Examples of the flexibility of this formula can be found on the sample form.

The **formula for manufacturers** will help you determine a wholesale value for your product. You will need to compute the cost of your labor. Figure the amount of time needed to make one item and the hourly wage to be paid for its production. Be realistic! What would you pay a contract laborer or an employee? Now determine the cost of materials for making one unit. Figure how many units one person could produce per year. Estimate your annual overhead and your desired annual profit.

The formula is the **cost of labor** plus the **cost of materials for one unit** times the **number of units to be produced in one year**. Add this amount to the **annual overhead plus the desired annual profit**. Now divide that quantity by the **number of units to be produced in one year**. This will give you the wholesale price you must charge to reach your desired annual income. Refer to the sample **Formula for Manufacturers Worksheet** at the end of this chapter. The following data has been used to compute the rate:

> Cost of labor per item = $2.50
> (Compute the amount of time needed to make one item.
> In the example, one half hour. Figure the hourly wage.
> In this case, $5.00. The cost of labor per item would
> be $2.50)
>
> Cost of materials for one unit = $2.00
>
> Number of units produced per year = 2,000
>
> Estimated annual overhead = $4,000
>
> Desired annual profit = $10,000

Most stores will **keystone** or double the wholesale price to arrive at a retail price. Since your wholesale price is $11.50, you can assume a retail price of $23.00. Perhaps this is too high for the consumer. You may want to consider adjusting some of the figures you are using. Examples of the flexibility of this formula are shown on the sample form.

These formulas and examples are offered as guides in helping you in determining your wholesale product price and hourly service rate. They are only as accurate as the figures being used.

The only significant profit is net profit after taxes. It is a common misconception that "the more you sell, the more you'll make." Profits are tied directly to both sales and costs. Any change in either will affect the profit. Increased sales can lead to increased profits as long as costs are kept under control. The best possible situation would be to increase sales while decreasing costs. This is the goal of every entrepreneur.

Customer Acceptance of a price is based on supply and demand, economic and psychological considerations.

Customers are willing to pay more for products or services that have a limited availability. Seasonal, fad, unusual, and imported items can usually command a higher price because of their inherent higher value and desirability. Customers generally will not accept higher prices unless extra services such as gift wrapping, free alterations, or free delivery are provided.

As long as you can cover your costs, you can set your prices according to the biggest return in terms of what the traffic can bear.

RESOURCES: PRICING

SMALL BUSINESS ADMINISTRATION

"What is the Best Selling Price?"
Management Aid 1.002

"Keep Pointed Toward Profit"
Management Aid 1.003

"Basic Budgets for Profit Planners"
Management Aid 1.004

"Pricing for Small Manufacturers"
Management Aid 1.005

CASH TO BE PAID OUT WORKSHEET
(CASH FLOWING OUT OF YOUR BUSINESS)

START-UP COSTS:
    Business License (annual expense) $_____
    DBA Filing Fee (one-time cost)   _____
    Other start-up costs:

    _____   _____
    _____   _____
    _____   _____

INVENTORY PURCHASES   _____
    Cash out for items for resale or services

SELLING EXPENSE (DIRECT EXPENSE)
    Advertising   _____
    Freight   _____
    Packaging Costs   _____
    Parts & Supplies   _____
    Sales Salaries   _____
    Misc. Direct Exp.   _____
TOTAL DIRECT EXPENSE   _____

OPERATING EXPENSE (INDIRECT EXPENSE)
    Depreciation Expense   _____
    Insurance   _____
    Licenses & Permits   _____
    Office Salaries   _____
    Rent Expense   _____
    Utilities   _____
    Miscell. Indirect Exp.   _____
TOTAL INDIRECT EXPENSE   _____

ASSETS (LONG-TERM PURCHASES)   _____
    Cash to be paid in current period

LIABILITIES   _____
    Cash outlay for retiring debts, loans,
    and/or accounts payable

OWNER EQUITY   _____
    Cash to be withdrawn by owner

        TOTAL CASH TO BE PAID OUT . . . . . $_____

Note: Be sure to use the same time period throughout your worksheets--- monthly, quarterly annually.

HOURLY RATE FORMULA

$$\frac{\text{Desired Annual Net Income}}{\text{No. Working Hours per Year}} + \frac{\text{Annual Expenses}}{\text{No. Working Hours per Year}}$$

BASE FIGURES:
  Desired annual net income = $10,000
  No. Working hours per year = 1,000   = $18.00/hr.
  Annual overhead = $8,000

LOWER OVERHEAD:
  Desired annual net income = $10,000
  No. Working hours per year = 1,000   = $16.00/hr.
  Annual overhead = $6,000

MORE HOURS:
  Desired annual net income = $10,000
  No. Working hours per year = 1500   = $12.00/hr.
  Annual overhead = $8,000

Note: Unit costs may drop as the production increases due to quantity buying. Overhead costs will increase due to employee expenses when the work force is increased.

FORMULA FOR MANUFACTURERS

$$\frac{\text{No. of units produced per year} \times [\text{Cost of labor} + \text{Materials for 1 unit}] + \text{Estimated Annual Overhead} + \text{Desired Annual Profit}}{\text{Number of Units per Year}}$$

BASE FIGURES:
    Cost of labor = $2.50
    Cost of materials = $2.00 per unit
    No. units per year = 2,000   =$11.50 wholesale price
    Est. annual overhead = $4,000
    Desired annual profit = $10,000

INCREASE PRODUCTION:
    Cost of labor = $2.50
    Cost of materials = $2.00 per unit
    No. units per year = 4,000   =$8.00 wholesale price
    Est. annual overhead $4,000
    Desired annual profit = $10,000

MORE PROFIT:
    Cost of labor = $2.50
    Cost of materials = $2.00 per unit
    No. units per year = 2,000   =$14.00 wholesale price
    Est. annual overhead = $4,000
    Desired annual profit = $15,000

MORE PROFIT THROUGH MORE EMPLOYEES
    Cost of labor = $2.50
    Cost of materials = $2.00 per unit
    No. units per year = 6,000   =$7.66 wholesale price
    Est. annual overhead = $4,000
    Desired annual profit = $15,000

Note: As employees are hired, the employer expense portion of your overhead may increase. With increased production, the cost of materials may drop because of quantity buying. Take this into consideration and adjust your figures accordingly.

9

PACKAGE DESIGN

9 PACKAGE DESIGN

Packaging serves two purposes: It protects the product and it conveys an image. Consumers often decide to purchase a product based on the appeal of the package that encloses it. Attractive packaging can also lead to impulse buying.

In order to keep costs down, companies just starting out should use stock packaging rather than having it custom-designed. When cash flow is not a problem and the product is established, you may customize the packaging.

The selection of stock packaging has greatly improved in the past few years. Look through the trade magazines of the packaging industry for supplier listings and ads. These publications will cover new techniques and materials available. You may attend Trade Shows in order to look at samples and review prices. The **Thomas Register** (a library reference) and the Yellow Page Directory will list packaging suppliers.

An extension of packaging is store display. If you have a fragile item, you may want to provide a display unit. It is well worth the cost if it saves the merchandise.

Become familiar with the materials needed in specialized areas such as food handling and with tamper-proof devices.

Consider product liability, bar codes, shape, and materials. Can your package be opened without the customer injuring himself? Many retail stores will not handle your products without a bar code. Shape is important. Storage areas and shelf space are designed for square or rectangular packaging. Materials must be chosen carefully. Some types of plastic deteriorate and become yellow and brittle with improper storage.

The package itself can be used as an advertising medium. Packaging and labeling are forms of direct communication with the consumer. The expansion of self-serve shopping has placed increased emphasis on packaging. The package must convince the shopper to buy a particular product over that of a competitor.

The Fair Packaging and Labeling Act (FPLA) is the primary Federal law requiring mandatory labeling provisions for all packaged consumer commodities and outlining labeling provisions. The Food and Drug Administration has regulatory authority for enforcing the FPLA as it relates to food, drugs, cosmetics, and therapeutic devices. The Federal Trade Commission has authority for all other consumer commodities. The packaging and labeling guidelines for your area of concern can be obtained by contacting the governmental agencies listed at the end of this section.

Various transportation companies have standards and requirements that must be taken into account. Consider size, weight, and strength of the shipping carton.

The time you spend in designing your packaging and researching the materials to be used will be time well spent.

RESOURCES: PACKAGE DESIGN

OFFICE OF CONSUMER AFFAIRS
U. S. Department of Commerce
Washington, D.C. 20230

> "Advertising, Packaging, & Labeling"
> "Product Warranties and Servicing"
> "Consumer Product Safety"

FEDERAL TRADE COMMISSION
Pennsylvania Avenue & 6th Street N.W.
Washington, D.C. 20580

FOOD AND DRUG ADMINISTRATION
Department of Health & Human Services
5600 Fisher Lane
Rockville, MD 20857

10

METHODS OF DISTRIBUTION

10 METHODS OF DISTRIBUTION

Independent business organizations are available to provide a flow of products and services from the marketer to the market. They fall into two catagories: resellers and facilitating businesses.

Resellers are the wholesalers and the retailers. They are the people we call the "middlemen." They operate between you, as the manufacturer or supplier, and the customer.

They may take the form of a **manufacturer's representative** who will handle your product and represent it to the retailer through trade show exposure or direct contact through sales reps. Sales reps usually carry a line of related, but not competitive products. They cover specific territories. Reps work strictly on commission and receive a percentage of the wholesale price. You must furnish the sales materials: price lists, brochures, sample sets. You must have a written contract specifying the territory, the terms of sale, commission percentage, and terms of contract.

Once you have established a working relationship with a rep, work closely. Let him know when you have a new product or design. Let him know ahead of time if you anticipate delivery delays. He would rather hear it from you than from the customer.

Reps are excellent sources of information regarding trends in your field. Their ideas are based on the demands observed in the marketplace.

Trade journals and directories of manufacturer's reps will give you listings of resellers covering your field. A resource listing follows this chapter.

A **retailer** may act as the "middle man" between you and your product. You may represent yourself and sell directly to the retail outlet for a wholesale price plus shipping and handling.

Catalogs are another form of resale for your product. We now see specialty catalogs for sale at chain bookstores. Home television shopping shows find merchandise through catalogs.

Review catalogs and see if your product would be appropriate for addition to their line. You may be asked to pay a fee for being included or you may pay a percentage on sales. Catalogs have become big business. If your market analysis indicates that your customers purchase by mail, by all means, contact the catalog company with that information and include sales information on your product.

The second entity available to aid you in getting your product or service to the customer is the **facilitating business**. They provide transportation and warehousing of goods between seller and buyer. They deal with the physical distribution of goods.

A major part of the physical distribution system involves direct shipping of products to customers. The four major forms of **transportation** are railroads, trucks, ships, and airplanes. You must decide on the form of transportation to use and the particular carriers. Your goal is to move the right goods to the right place at the right time. Physical distribution costs are a substantial part of operating costs in many companies.

Each form of transportation is suited to a particular need. There are weight and size limitations for some carriers. The post office delivers anywhere in the world while United Parcel Service delivers in the continental U.S. and Hawaii. Ask about their particular packing requirements.

What are the shipping trends for your industry? How are goods shipped by the competition? Contact the Interstate Commerce Commission regarding guidelines and restrictions on your products.

Warehousing or storage involves the holding of goods from the time of their production to the time of their sale. Goods are frequently produced throughout the year but sold seasonally, thus requiring storage. Excess goods and goods purchased for later use must be stored. The types of merchandise that may require storage differ widely.

Warehouses are the most common type of storage facility. They may be privately owned or public warehouses. Public warehouses are regulated by the government. The Chamber of Commerce in your community will be able to give you information on warehouse facilities.

You may find it more cost effective to operate on a "do-it-yourself" basis. When starting out, you may wish to deal directly with retailers and customers and provide your own warehousing in a small self-storage location.

RESOURCES: METHODS OF DISTRIBUTION

MANUFACTURERS' AGENTS NATIONAL ASSOCIATION

> Agent & Representative Company
> 626 N. Garfield Avenue
> Alhambra, CA 98101
>
> > Publishes a geographical and alphabetical directory of association members along with information about lines and territories handled.

U.S. DEPARTMENT OF COMMERCE
Office of Consumer Affairs
Washington, DC 20233

Interstate Commerce Commission
Federal Trade Commission

LOCATION

Market
Supplies
Labor Force
Transportation
Competition
Cost
Home-based
Shopping Centers
Incubators

11 LOCATION

General factors must be considered when deciding on a business location. Among them are accessibility to the market, location of the competition, source of supplies, availability of a labor force, means of transportation, and cost. Other considerations are zoning regulations, area crime rates, and neighborhood image.

Your most important consideration in choosing a location is being able to satisfy the market. They must be able to reach your business easily, safely, and pleasantly. One of the most effective ways to evaluate location is to do a **map analysis**. Make a map of the area in which you wish to locate. You may enlarge a section of an existing map by using a copier with an enlarging feature, or you may draw your own. Have a copy shop run off some duplicates and one transparency. On the transparency, indicate the location sites available within your target area and mark them with a colored pen or assign each of them a number. You will be coding information onto the duplicate maps. You will be able to place the transparency over the coded map in order to get a feeling for each site. For instance, take one of the duplicate maps to the police department. Ask about area crime rates. Shade the high crime area on your map. When you place the transparency over the duplicate, you will be able to see if any of your potential locations fall in that area.

MARKET

On another duplicate map, shade in the areas in which your target market lives, shops or works. Again use the transparency overlay and see if your customers will be able to reach you easily. Is there freeway access, good traffic flow, and adequate parking? Customers are concerned about safety. Can they reach your place of business with a feeling of security? Your crime rate map will show if they have to pass through a high crime area. Their trip to your establishment should be a pleasant one. Drive around and walk the routes your customers will take. Get a feeling for the neighborhood.

A **Location Analysis Worksheet** has been provided for your use at the end of this chapter. Fill one out and use it in conjunction with your area maps for a thorough site evaluation.

SUPPLIES

Mark the sources of your raw materials on a map. If you are in the retail or service business, can suppliers reach you easily? Are there one-way streets and confusing traffic patterns? If you are a manufacturer, locate your sources of supply. Would it be more cost effective to locate near your raw materials?

LABOR FORCE

Your next consideration is the availability of employees. Some areas do not have an adequate group of people to form a labor pool. The prevailing wage rate in the area may be out of line with competitor's rates in other areas. The Chamber of Commerce will be able to give you this type of information.

TRANSPORTATION

Consider traffic flow during peak hours. Will customers be able to reach your business? What are the bus routes? Can your target market reach you on public transportation?

Not only are you concerned about your accessibility for customers and suppliers, you want to know future plans for the area in terms of transportation. Visit the City Planning and Public Works Departments. Are there future plans for road construction? Will any streets be changed to one-way? Will a new freeway be built which will take traffic flow away from your location? Are new parking facilities planned? Will new parking regultations be enforced? All of these considerations could have a negative effect on your business.

COMPETITION

How many similar businesses are located nearby? What does their sales volume appear to be? Use one of your maps to locate the competition.

COST

Office space for minimal rent is not always the best. There usually is a reason why the rent is low. Find out why the space is available, how long it has been vacant, and the history of the previous tenants. If there has been a frequent turnover, it may be considered a "bad location". The Chamber of Commerce can give you information on average square footage costs for your area.

Check with the Zoning Commission regarding any rezoning planned for the surrounding area. Walk around the area. Does it project the image you have for your business?

HOME-BASED BUSINESS

There are advantage to locating your business in your home. You can save on commute costs. The **home-based business** is a practical solution for the parent with child care concerns. The Internal Revenue Service and your local Zoning Commission have strict guidelines for home business.

One of the disadvantages of a home business is the difficulty in projecting a professional image. There will also be family interruptions. You may feel a psychological need to separate home and business. Usually a home office doesn't allow much room for growth.

Some other considerations in a home-based business are distances to suppliers and customers, locations of competitors, future business goals, type of neighborhood, insurance requirements, and zoning regulations. Zoning laws vary with each city and are mainly concerned with the potential for increased traffic flow, noise pollution, and the change of the character of the neighborhood.

SHOPPING CENTERS

You may consider locating in a **shopping center**. These sites are pre-planned as merchandising units. On-site parking is available. Customers can drive in, park, and shop with speed and safety. You can take advantage of customers drawn to the area by other stores.

There are some limitations you should know about. You will be part of a merchant team and must pay your pro rata share of the budget. You must keep store hours, light your windows, and place your signs within established guidelines.

INCUBATORS

A new entity is emerging in the location market - the **business incubator** facility. To reduce overhead costs for new businesses, the incubator program offers a number of services to tenants through a centralized resource station. Usually included in the tenant package are reception and telephone answering, maintenance, conference room facilities, and shipping and receiving. Other services may include complete clerical services at a nominal charge.

Incubator facilities are targeted toward small start-up and new firms. Square footage costs are low. The new businesses are expected to remain for 2 to 3 years. At that point it is hoped they will be successful enough to move out into another location.

Evaluate the possibilities of the home-based business, the shopping center location, and the business incubator in terms of your enterprise. Carefully analyze all of the factors we have discussed in this chapter. The location of your business can well mean the difference between success and failure.

RESOURCES: LOCATION

SMALL BUSINESS ADMINISTRATION

> "Locating and Relocating Your Business"
> Management Aid 2.002
> "Factors to Consider in a Shopping Center Location"
> Management Aid 2.017
> "Using a Traffic Study to Select a Retail Site"
> Management Aid 2.021
> "Store Location: Little Things Mean a Lot"
> Management Aid 2.024

LOCATION ANALYSIS WORKSHEET

1. ADDRESS:

2. NAME OF REALTOR/CONTACT PERSONS:

3. FORMER TENANT & REASON FOR LEAVING:

4. SQUARE FOOTAGE/COST:

5. PERSONAL INSPECTION DISCOVERIES:

6. NOTES FROM WALKING TOUR OF AREA:

7. NEIGHBORING SHOPS:

8. ZONING REGULATIONS:

9. TRAFFIC PATTERNS:
    for customers -

    for suppliers -

10. ADDITIONAL INFORMATION:

NOTE: Keep up with changes in the zoning regulations, the traffic patterns, and the business and character of the neighborhood in your location.

12

TIMING OF MARKET ENTRY

12 TIMING OF MARKET ENTRY

You won't find much written on timing of market entry and yet it is critical to the success of your business. It is not wise to present your business to the market just because you are ready. It takes careful planning and research.

Having your products and services available at the right time and the right place is more a matter of understanding your customers than of your organizational schedule.

Many businesses are seasonal in nature. Since most games are purchased for Christmas gifts, the board game example we used previously would best be introduced in September and October in order to be established by the Christmas season. The marketing schedule for the gift industry is different from that of a business that sells throughout the year.

Food purchasing usually takes place around the end of the week. This is why most in-store food taste tests are done on Friday, Saturday, and Sunday. Payday is usually at the end of the week on a biweekly schedule. Offer your take-home or delivered "home-cooked" food on Friday when you know your target market has been paid, is tired at the end of the week, is hungry, and doesn't want to cook! A satisfied customer will call you at other times during the week.

The reception of new products and services can be affected by the seasons, the weather, and the holidays. Early January and early September seem to be the best times to mail flyers and catalogs. The holiday season is over and consumers are receptive to the new year and new ideas in early January. By early September, vacations have been taken and children are back in school. There is more time available to look at printed material.

The major gift shows are held in the summer months (June, July, and August) and again in January and February. Most wholesale buying takes place at these shows. You will want to present your products to a manufacturer's representative well before these dates. November and December are not good months for introducing new service businesses unless they relate in some way to the holiday season. The spring is a better time to introduce a new service business.

Each marketer must adjust his timing of market entry according to the nature of his business and his customers. Information from the trade journals and trade associations in your field will give you the information you need regarding the timing patterns of your industry.

RESOURCES: TIMING OF MARKET ENTRY

Encyclopedia of Associations: Provides information on every major trade and professional association in the U.S. A library reference.

National Trade and Professional Association of the U.S.
Directory published by Columbia Books, Inc., Washington, D.C.

ADVERTISING YOUR BUSINESS

**Media Advertising
Displays
Community Involvement
Networking
Tradeshows & Exhibits
Direct Mail
Telemarketing
Yellow Pages
Discounts
Promotional Gimmicks**

13 ADVERTISING YOUR BUSINESS

Advertising is defined by Webster as "printed or spoken matter that tells about or praises a product or service publicly so as to make people want to buy it." Advertising is a natural extension of your marketing research and plan. It is the means for getting information about your product or service to the buying public. There are a variety of ways to accomplish this. Surprisingly, all of the methods mentioned in this chapter are easily accessible, even to the small or home-based business.

By now you will have identified what is **unique** about your business and how that uniqueness will **benefit the customer**. This theme or image for your product or service will carry through all of your advertising. It's what sets you apart from the competition and it's what will attract the customer.

Find the inherent drama in what you are doing. Create an interest. Transfer that inherent drama into a meaningful benefit. Consumers are attracted by benefits.

MEDIA ADVERTISING

Media coverage refers to paid advertising in newspaper, on radio, and on television and to publicity obtained through interviews and articles.

Newspaper advertising usually reaches a large audience, has a short life span, is relatively inexpensive, and is quickly and easily changed. Tailor your ad to the editorial "mood" of the paper. Determine what special feature sections are being planned. If the business of desktop publishing will be featured in a special section and you are opening a mobile repair service for such equipment, you will want to advertise in that section. Your ad can be placed to reach a selected audience. The cost of the ad will vary according to frequency of publication and area of circulation. Ads are available in various sizes and in several formats such as display or classified ads.

In addition to paid advertising, don't overlook **publicity**. Publicity is information about you and your product or service and it is free. You can call the Business Editor or Feature Editor of a widely - circulated newspaper in your area and explain your product or service. Before calling, consider what is unique about you and your business. Stress that uniqueness in order to convince the editor that such an article would be of interest to his readers. There are two approaches that can be used when seeking publicity. The first is to request an **interview** either at the newspaper office or in your place of business. The second is to suggest that you **contribute a newspaper article**, complete with photos, telling about some aspect of your business. If one newspaper isn't interested, call another. Don't be afraid to approach the media. You are the best advertising that you can get. A **sample press release form** has been included at the end of this chapter.

Analyze the advertising of your competition regarding size, placement, and frequency. Your questionnaires will have indicated the newspapers read by your target market. Those are the ones in which you will place your advertising.

Radio advertising is usually local, reaches a preselected audience, can be changed frequently, is limited to brief copy, is relatively expensive and can be repeated frequently. It is priced according to length of message, time of broadcast, and frequency of broadcast. It is either read live by broadcasters or taped in advance.

There are two types of radio programming: background and foreground. **Background programs** are on the music stations. **Foreground programs** are on the news/talk stations. Foreground programs involve a more active listener. They will probably pay more attention to your commercials.

It has been proven that you must catch the listener's attention in the first 3 seconds. Your ad will be done live or taped in advance. The three biggest complaints about radio commercials are that they are noisy, they have idiotic humor, and they lack sincerity. Keep that in mind if you write your own commercial. Be simple and straightforward. Another approach to radio coverage of your business would be to offer your service as an expert in your field on a radio talk show. You can answer questions from listeners on your business.

Television advertising reaches large marketing areas, is relatively expensive, and is limited to brief copy. This form of advertising is usually highly professional and is priced according to length of message, time of broadcast, frequency of broadcast, time of year, and whether or not the station is an independent or a member of a network.

Cost of advertising is based on gross rating points (GRP). One point equals 1% of the television sets in the TV marketing area. The GRP unit cost is determined by the competitive situation, size of area, and time of year. Advertising costs may be higher during the holiday season which is considered to be October through December.

Prime time covers the period from 8:00 p.m. to 11:00 p.m. and is more costly. The "fringe time" before and after prime time may be more cost-effective for you.

Find out what shows your market watches. The television station will have demographic and psychographic breakdowns on their viewing audience. Most use market studies to effectively help position advertising where it will be seen by those interested in the products or service offered.

Television rates are negotiable. You may wish to use the services of a media-buying service. Their average fee is 5% of your rates, they deal in volume, and can save you money.

Don't discount Cable Television. This medium is becoming very useful to the small business owner.

If television advertising costs won't fit into your budget, consider approaching the television news department from the publicity point of view. Call the stations in your area. Ask which shows have guests. Ask for the name of the person that is in charge of securing those guests. Follow up by contacting that person and promote yourself in a professional manner.

Your business may qualify for a Public Service Announcement (PSA). This is a good way to announce classes or to publicize any meetings at which you may be a guest speaker.

DISPLAYS, COMMUNITY INVOLVEMENT, AND NETWORKING

These entities offer other unique ways of getting the message about your business to your customers.

Displays may be set up at community-oriented functions such as city fairs, community events, and civic meetings. This is a good way to present your product or service to the buying public. You can also get valuable feedback.

Community involvement can be an effective means of advertising. Membership in civic organizations can pave the way to being a guest speaker. Active membership affords you an excellent opportunity for networking.

Networking is the exchange of ideas and information that takes place everyday in your life. You are going to direct that exchange to your benefit and to the benefit of those around you. The more you meet with people, the more you will be able to promote your business, to learn more about the business community around you, and to become more self-confident. Membership in civic and business organizations such as the Chamber of Commerce is an excellent means of accomplishing this.

TRADE SHOWS AND EXHIBITS

Participation in trade shows and exhibits allows you to take advantage of promotional campaigns that would be too expensive for a small business to undertake alone. You can request listings of trade events from malls and convention centers. Participation in trade shows and membership in trade organizations give you visibility in your business field. These shows are usually attended only by those interested in your particular field. This is an excellent way to reach your target market. You may choose to participate in a co-op display to cut costs.

DIRECT MAIL

Direct mail can be an effective way to deliver specific information in a personal way to large numbers of people. Direct mail can take the form of inexpensive fact sheets, letters, promotional give-aways, contests, discount coupons, and brochures.

Brochures are essential for any business for which a prospective customer needs detailed information. More information can be supplied in a brochure than would be practical in a classified ad. Brochures can be distributed through the mail, door-to-door, at fairs or mall events. An outline to help you develop a brochure has been included at the end of this section.

Direct mail has special uses. It can be used to solicit mail-order or phone-order business, to announce new products or services, to notify customers of price changes, to welcome new customers, to thank current customers, and to announce special events such as sales.

To be cost-effective, you must target your market. Rent a good list from a list broker. The principles of direct mail that were discussed in Chapter 3 also apply here. Please refer to that section for additional information.

TELEMARKETING

Even when personal selling is essential, it doesn't mean that you have to be standing in front of the customer. You can get the same results by phone. While some consumers resent the invasion of telephone sales calls into their homes, telemarketing can still be an effective tool. It can be used to contact new customers, to maintain contact with current customers, and to remind slow payers.

To be effective, telemarketing must be organized. Use targeted lists. Make a clear and specific offer. One advantage to telemarketing is that you will get an instant response.

The network and system you used to conduct your phone surveys can be put into operation to sell your product or service. Again, refer to Chapter 3 for more information on marketing by telephone

YELLOW PAGES

This is an effective means of advertising. Every person with a phone has a copy of the Yellow Pages. You have a captive audience: they are looking at the directory because they need what you have to offer.

It is the most widely used form of advertising. One small business owner states that in any given week, 50% of her customers are directed to her through the Yellow Pages.

The telephone company advertising staff is very knowledgeable and will give you help in designing an ad which will present your business in an effective manner. Be aware that directories are published at various times of the year. Call the phone company to determine publication deadlines.

DISCOUNTS

Discounts are an excellent way to get additional customers. Discounts can be given to customers who bring in referrals. They may also be offered through coupons and brochures. Everyone likes to think that they are saving money.

PROMOTIONAL GIMMICKS

This advertising medium may take the form of T-shirts, pens, key rings, plastic shopping bags, calendars, balloons, and bumper stickers. The most effective gimmicks are useful items. The gimmick should be appropriate to the business it's representing. For example, a logo or business name on a T-shirt is an effective way of advertising a business dealing with the out-of doors, such as a bicycle shop or a kite maker. Pens would be good for someone who manufactures notecards and stationery. Balloons could represent a company specializing in children's items. Be creative in your use of this advertising form.

SUMMARY

As a new business, your advertising budget will probably be limited. Deciding how much money to spend to advertise your product or service can be one of your most difficult decisions. Advertising costs are an investment in your company's future. Choose the methods that will best reach your target market.

The forms of advertising chosen must be evaluated for effectiveness. To help you with this analysis, an **Advertising Response Record** has been included at the end of this section. From this information, determine which has been the most effective means of advertising for your business. Eliminate those methods which have not proven effective and transfer those funds to increase your advertising in the area which will give you the best results.

After evaluating the different methods of advertising, work up an individual plan for your business. A sample plan for **Ocean Adventures** has been included at the end of this chapter.

RESOURCES: ADVERTISING YOUR BUSINESS

Levinson, Jay, **Guerrilla Marketing**, Houghton Mifflin Co., Boston, 1984

SMALL BUSINESS ADMINISTRATION

"Advertising Guidelines for Small Retail Firms"
Management Aid 4.015
"Signs in Your Business"
Management Aid 4.016
"Planning Your Advertising Budget"
Management Aid 4.018
"Do You Know the Results of Your Advertising"
Management Aid 4.020
"Specialty Advertising for Small Business"
Management Aid 4.021

DIRECT MAIL/MARKETING ASSOCIATION
6 E. 43rd Street
New York, NY 10017

PRESS RELEASE FORM

SOURCE INFORMATION

Name, address, phone number
of person to call for more info.

RELEASE DATE

for immediate release or
specify date to be published

HEADLINE
(Centered in Capital Letters)

BASIC FACTS
(Who, What, When, Were, Why, How)

FOR MORE INFORMATION: Be sure to include name and address and/or phone number at the end of the article so that the reader can obtain additional information.

-30-
(Signifies end of article)

DEVELOPING A BROCHURE

A **brochure** is a general term for promotional material which tells the following about your business:

1. The business name.

2. **The business address.** Be sure to include the full address and zip code.

3. **Telephone number.** Be sure to include the area code.

4. **Name of the contact person.** Customers prefer to ask for an individual when they call.

5. Photos or drawings of your product or a representation of your service.

6. Description of your product or service.

7. **Price list.** Indicate if it is the wholesale or retail list.

8. Terms of payment.
    a. **Net 30:** Invoice must be paid in full within 30 days.
    b. **Net 30, 2%/10:** Invoice to be paid in full in 30 days. If paid within 10 days, 2% discount can be taken on the bill excluding shipping charges.
    c. **C.O.D:** Invoice is paid to the delivery agent on receipt of goods.
    d. **ProForma:** Goods will be shipped after receipt of full payment.

9. **Return Policy:** "Returns and/or adjustments must be made within 14 days of receipt of goods." Use time frame of your choice.

10. **Shipping Terms:** F.O.B. Origin would mean that the customer pays shipping charges and assumes the responsibility for the goods from the time they leave your business. **Example: F.O.B. Fullerton, CA.**

11. **Minimum Order Policy:** Can be a dollar or unit amount.

12. **Warranties and/or Guarantees.**

ADVERTISING RESPONSE RECORD

TYPE OF AD	DATE RUN	COST	CIRCULATION	NO. RESPONSES	INCOME GENERATED

Advertising your Business

ADVERTISING IDEAS FOR OCEAN ADVENTURES

RADIO: Contact local radio stations and ask for their procedure in securing talk show guests. Inform them of your area of expertise and stress the uniqueness of what you offer and the high interest of the public in what your business is doing. Suggest that you can relate kayaking experiences you have had and would enjoy taking listener calls.

NEWSPAPER: Contact the Sports Editor, Business Editor, Travel Editor and slant your article idea according to their areas of interest. The Sports Editor would be interested in an article about "The Sport of Ocean Kayaking". The Business Editor may want to cover a new and unique business developing within the area covered by his newspaper. The Travel Editor will be interested in an article entitled, "Kayaking to Baja". Have black and white photos available of the different aspects of your business.

Consider publishing an ad in the business section. Trained people at the newspaper can advise you about placement and size of ad. Be prepared to give the who, what, why, where, and how of the class or trip you will be offering.

TELEVISION: Contact television studios in your area and inquire about their format for securing talk show guests. Suggest that you could demonstrate the use of a kayak for their viewers, tell about trips you have taken, and demonstrate safety techniques. Perhaps, the host would be willing to be televised while taking a basic lesson!

Cable television also offers opportunities for coverage and less expensive advertising. Explore this resource.

Public Broadcasting Stations often have televised auctions as fund-raisers. Consider donating your Basic Paddling Course as one of the items offered for auction. This would be invaluable advertising.

DISPLAY: Create a display featuring photos of your trips and classes, copies of any publicity you have received, a kayak and the gear related to using, and have plenty of brochures and business cards on hand. Be prepared to answer questions regarding your business. Community affairs such as fairs and festivals usually offer space for this type of display. This format can also be used as an **EXHIBIT** at trade shows such as a Travel Show or Sports and Boating Show. These larger events are usually held in sports arenas or convention facilities.

COMMUNITY INVOLVEMENT: Join the Chamber of Commerce! This excellent group will afford you a forum for speaking as well as being a great networking group.

Consider working with a **Scout Council.** You could counsel in kayaking, water safety, and/or marine studies. This offers a new area for networking.

Look into teaching through the **YMCA**. Basic skills courses could be taught through the Y with a discount given to Y students who continue study.

BROCHURE: Make your message personal and stress your product or service. A brochure should show how your business is different from the competition and stress the advantages of dealing with you to the customer (see brochure in this section).

YELLOW PAGES AD: Yellow page advertising does work! Discuss placement and category with the staff in the Advertising Department of the Yellow Pages. They will be able to advise you.

PROMOTIONAL GIMMICKS: T-shirts with your name and logo could be given to those attending your classes and going on your trips. This would seem to be an appropriate promotional tool; active, outdoor people wear t-shirts and you will get good exposure this way.

Advertising is a continuing process. Be prepared to follow up on all leads. Have brochures ready to be mailed when you receive an inquiry. People get distracted and lose interest if their requests aren't handled promptly. Consider discounts for groups and referrals.

SUMMARY

SUMMARY

You've surveyed the market and examined trends as you have looked for a new product or service. You've written a disclosure letter, started a journal and explored the protection offered through copyright, trademark, and patent. Questionnaires have been composed, distributed, and evaluated in order to get a profile of your target market and a response to your idea. You've prepared a prototype and done some market testing. Evaluation of the competition has helped you determine what is unique about your business and how it will benefit the customer. By putting together your demographic and psychographic findings, you have zeroed in on the target market. You've positioned your product or service and prepared to enter the market. Pricing, package design, and location have been considered. Careful thought has been given to timing of market entry. You have researched all the methods of advertising. You have done your **market research**.

Market research is an orderly, objective way of learning about products and services and the people who buy them. Research is limited only by your imagination. Much of it can be done with very little cost except your time and mental effort.

The natural extention of market research is the **marketing plan**. A market plan is your own guide to what you hope to accomplish and how you hope to accomplish it. It's the blueprint of your marketing program and will keep you on the right track.

We hope that this book has given you some practical information and has motivated you to get your idea **OUT OF YOUR MIND....AND INTO THE MARKETPLACE**™!

FOR MORE INFORMATION

FOR MORE INFORMATION

BUREAU OF CONSUMER PROTECTION
Division of Special Statutes
6th and Pennsylvania Ave., N.W.
Washington, DC 20580

> Write for information related to your specific business

CONSUMER PRODUCTS SAFETY COMMISSION
Bureau of Compliance
5401 Westbard Avenue
Bethesda, MD 20207

> Request catalog of booklets available. For Example:
> **The Federal Hazardous Substances Act**
> **Consumer Product Safety Act of 1972**
> **Flammable Fabrics Act**

FEDERAL TRADE COMMISSION
Division of Legal and Public Records
Washington, DC 20580

> Request trade practice rules applicable to your business. For Example:
> **The Jewelry Industry**
> **The Hand Knitting Yarn Industry**

FOOD AND DRUG ADMINISTRATION
5600 Fishers Lane
Rockville, MD 20857

> Send for requirements governing packaging and labeling of food and food-related products.

INTERNAL REVENUE SERVICE
Washington, DC 20224

>Request list of publications such as:
>**Tax Guide for Small Business #334**
>**Business Use of Your Home #587**

MANUFACTURER'S AGENTS NATIONAL ASSOCIATION
Agent and Representative Company
626 N. Garfield Avenue
Alhambra, CA 98101

>Publishers a geographical and alphabetical directory of association members along with information about lines and territories handled.

NATIONAL ALLIANCE OF HOME-BASED BUSINESSWOMEN (NAHB)
P.O. Box 306
Midland Park, NJ 07432

>Professional, political, and economic information for the home-based business person. Membership includes newsletter, **Alliance**, listing in annual directory, and networking opportunities. Request membership information, publications list, and copy of **Model Zoning Ordinance**.

SUPERINTENDENT OF DOCUMENTS
U.S. Government Printing Office
Washington, DC 20402

>Request subject bibliography listings. There are fees for most publications. Sample titles are:
>**For Women: Managing Your Own Business**
>**Handbook for Small Business**
>**Managing for Profits**
>**Inventory Management**
>**Evaluating Money Sources**

U.S. DEPARTMENT OF COMMERCE
Office of Consumer Affairs
Washington, DC 20233

> Offers free booklets such as:
> **Produce Warranties**
> **Advertising, Packaging, and Labeling**

U.S. DEPARTMENT OF LABOR
200 Constitution Avenue, N.W.
Washington, DC 20210

> Request catalog of publications such as:
> **Raising Money and Running Your Own Business**

U.S. SMALL BUSINESS ADMINISTRATION
1441 L Street, N.W.
Washington, DC 20416

> Request order forms and listings for the SBA series called **Management Aids, Starting Out Series,** and **Small Business Bibliographies.** There is a small charge for most publications. Sample listings follow:
> **The ABC's of Borrowing MA 1.001**
> **What is the Best Selling Price? MA 1.002**
> **Getting the Facts about Income Tax Reporting MA 1.014**
> **Keeping Records in Small Business MA 1.017**
> **Business Plan for Small Manufacturer's MA 2.007**
> **Factors in Considering a Shopping Center Location MA 2.017**
> **Home Business SBB 2**
> **Ideas into Dollars (Inventors' Guide) SBB 91**
> **Selling by Mail Order SOS 0149**
> **Radio-Television Repair Shop SOS 0104**
> **Starting an Independent Consulting Practice SOS 0204**

INDEX

INDEX

A

active business 13
address code 25
advertising 41, 71
Advertising Plan 100, 101
Advertising Response Record 99
ADVERTISING YOUR BUSINESS 91-101
age distribution 46

B

background program 92
bar codes 71
benefit the customer 41, 91
brochures 93, 98
business incubator 83
buying style 47

C

Cable Television 92
Cash to be Paid Out Worksheet 61, 65
catalogs 76
Census Bureau 46
Chamber of Commerce 39, 46, 76, 82, 93
coding log 29
community involvement 47, 93
competition 23, 39, 82
Competition Evaluation Form 42
copyright 13, 16
cost 61, 82
crime rates 81
customer acceptance 63

D

demographics 45, 92
Department of Commerce 48, 77
Depository Library Program 15
direct competition 39
direct expenses 61
direct mail 24, 93
Direct Mail/Marketing Association 26, 95
disclosure document 16
disclosure letter 13
discount coupons 23, 94
discounts 94
displays 93
distribution 23

E

education 46
ethnic origin 46
evaluate current buying trends 7
evaluating a competitive product 40
EVALUATING THE COMPETITION 39-41
evaluating the competitive service 40
evaluation of the response 25
exhibits 93

F

facilitating business 76
fads 7
family status 46
Federal Trade Commission 35, 72
FINDING YOUR TARGET MARKET 45-52
finding the competition 39
fixed expenses 61
flyers 93, 98
Food and Drug Administration 73
FOR MORE INFORMATION 107-111
foreground programs 92
format for questionnaires 21
Formula for Manufacturers 61, 67

G

gift shows 65, 87
gross rating points 92
group interviews 25

H

home-based business 82
Hourly Rate Formula 61, 66
HOW TO SURVEY THE MARKET 7-9

I

image 39, 57, 71
income 46
incubators 83
indirect competition 39
infringement 16
interference 16
Interstate Commerce Commission 76
interview 25, 91
Inventors Shows 8, 9

115

J

journal 13, 16

K

keystone 41, 63

L

labor force 82
letters of reference 34
lifestyle 47
LOCATION 81-83
Location Analysis Worksheet 84
log 13

M

mailing lists 24, 94
manufacturer's representative 75, 77
map analysis 81
market research 47, 81, 105
Marketing Research Worksheet 30
materials 71
media advertising 91
METHODS OF DISTRIBUTION 75-77
middlemen 75
mock-up 33

N

networking 93
new products 8
new services 8
newspaper advertising 91

O

occupation 46
operating expenses 61

P

PACKAGE DESIGN 71-72
packaging 71
passive business 13

P (Con't)

patents 15
personal behavior 47
personal interview 25
personal observation 7
population 45
population size 45
positioning 57
POSITIONING YOUR PRODUCT OR SERVICE 57
press release form 97
price 40, 61
PRICING 61-68
pricing formulas 61
product liability 71
production model 33
profit 62. 63
promotional gimmicks 95
PROTECTING YOUR IDEA 13-17
prototype 33
psychographics 47, 92
Public Service Announcement 93
publicity 91, 93
putting it together 47

Q

questionnaire 21, 27, 28, 47
questions about the competition 23

R

radio advertising 92
REACHING YOUR TARGET MARKET 53-95
RESEARCHING THE MARKET 3-52
resellers 75
retailer 75

S

S.C.O.R.E. 1, 49
self-concept 47
sex 46
shopping center 83
Small Business Administration 8, 17, 35, 41, 83, 95
store display 71
SUMMARY 105
supplies 81

T

target market 45, 81
Target Market Worksheet 51
telemarketing 24, 94
telephone surveys 24
television 92
television advertising 92
test marketing 34
testing a product 34
testing a service 34
TESTING THE MARKET 33-35
THE USE OF QUESTIONNAIRES 21-30
Thomas Register 71
TIMING OF MARKET ENTRY 87-88
trade journals 7, 9, 39, 87
Trade Shows 53. 70
trade shows and exhibits 93
trademark 15
transportation 76, 82
trends 7, 75
types of information 22

U

unique 41, 91
U.S. Department of Commerce 8, 9
U.S. Small Business Administration 8, 17, 35, 41, 83, 95

W

Warehousing 76
working model 33

Y

Yellow pages 39, 71, 94

Z

Zoning Commission 82
zoning regulations 82

OTHER BOOKS BY LINDA PINSON AND JERRY JINNETT

OUT OF YOUR MIND....AND INTO THE MARKET PLACE - a step-by-step guide for starting and succeeding with a small or home-based business.

ANATOMY OF A BUSINESS PLAN - presents a hands-on format for the reader in reseaching, writing, and putting to use a business plan for his company.

RECORDKEEPING: THE SECRET TO GROWTH AND PROFIT - Hands-on guide for setting up, analyzing, and understanding your business recordkeeping. Special section covering financial statement analysis

These books are available through your book store or directly from the publisher.